Oxfordshire's Lost Railwa

by

Peter Dale

The LMS station at Oxford Rewly Road, 1949.

Text © Peter Dale, 2004.
First published in the United Kingdom, 2004,
by Stenlake Publishing Ltd.
Telephone: 01290 551122
Printed by Cordfall Ltd., Glasgow G21 2QA

ISBN 1 84033 312 X

ACKNOWLEDGEMENTS

The publishers with to thank the following for contributing photographs
to this book: John Alsop for the front cover, pages 2, 4, 8, 9, 13–21, 23, 28,
30, 31, 33, 35, 36, 38–40, 42, 45, 48, and the back cover; and R.C. Casserley
for the inside front cover, pages 1, 3, 5–7, 10–12, 22, 24–27, 29, 32, 34, 37, 41,
43, 46, 47, and the inside back cover. The photograph on page 44 is from
the publishers' collection.

Chipping Norton Station.

INTRODUCTION

In railway terms Oxfordshire was dominated by the Great Western Railway. The first public railway in Oxfordshire was the part of the GWR main line between Reading and Steventon that entered the county near Goring and opened on 1 June 1840.

Early attempts to provide a railway to Oxford, branching from the GWR main line at Didcot were not successful and Oxford had to be content with the eight coaches a day that ran the 10 miles along the turnpike to and from Steventon. A bill passed in 1843 stipulated that the Oxford Railway, which ran to Oxford from a junction with the GWR at Didcot, should not carry any members of the University below the degrees of Master of Arts or Bachelor of Civil Law. The line opened on 12 June 1844.

North of Oxford there was considerable London & North Western Railway influence through the Oxford, Worcester & Wolverhampton Railway. This was originally proposed as a broad gauge line to link those places and became part of the Gauge War between the Great Western on the one hand and the Midland and LNWR on the other. The OW&W (often known as the 'Old Worse & Worse'!) opened as a narrow gauge line and when the LNWR opened a short branch from its Oxford line to the OW&W at Yarnton on 1 April 1854, trains to and from Worcester and Wolverhampton were routed by the longer LNWR route via Bletchley. The OW&W became part of the West Midland Railway by amalgamation and that in turn was absorbed by the Great Western in August 1863. From the end of September that year Worcester and Wolverhampton trains went to Paddington instead of Euston.

The Great Central Railway, which had a line to Banbury, evolved from the Manchester, Sheffield & Lincolnshire Railway when that company built its London extension and changed its name.

One other company's tracks could be seen in Oxfordshire: the line of the Stratford-upon-Avon & Midland Junction Railway (S&MJR) ran for about a mile in the northernmost corner of the county, between Fenny Compton and Byfield. The company's trains could also be seen at Banbury Merton Street.

It is worth adding a word of explanation here about the Grouping for non-railway enthusiasts. Many of the railways in Britain were built by small companies, sometimes with the backing of a larger company. In the years leading up to 1923 there was a process of consolidation by which smaller companies amalgamated or were absorbed by larger ones, but in 1922 there were still well over 100 different companies in Britain. In 1923 all but a few minor companies were grouped into four larger concerns by Act of Parliament. These were the Great Western Railway (which continued in an enlarged form), the Southern Railway, the London, Midland & Scottish Railway (LMS – which included the LNWR and S&MJR), and the London & North Eastern Railway (LNER – which included the Great Central). These four companies – often referred to as the 'Big Four' – continued until nationalisation in 1948.

Under British Railways a Modernisation Plan introduced in 1955 spelled the beginning of the end for steam on Britain's railways, while the Beeching Plan of 1963 saw the start of widespread closures of many minor, and some major, lines. One line in Oxfordshire bucked the trend: the LNWR line to Oxford reopened on 11 May 1987 and the station at Islip reopened on 13 May 1989.

Oxford was an interesting railway centre because it was possible to see locomotives of all the Big Four companies there. Southern locos worked in on trains from places such as Bournemouth and LNER locos worked in from Leicester or Nottingham besides the GWR and LMS locos.

It is hoped this book will rekindle memories of a slower, bygone age when the station was the natural starting point for any kind of journey and perhaps some will seek out the preserved lines throughout the country where scenes similar to these pictures are recreated. The preserved Chinnor & Princes Risborough Railway runs partly through Oxfordshire.

Thame Station, looking towards Princes Risborough.

Blenheim Branch

Passenger service withdrawn	1 March 1954	*Stations closed*	*Date*
Distance	3.7 miles	Blenheim & Woodstock	1 March 1954
Company	Woodstock Railway	Shipton-on-Cherwell Halt	1 March 1954

Blenheim & Woodstock Station.

Authorised by the Woodstock Railway Act of 25 September 1889, construction of this line began from a junction with the GWR main line 1 mile north of Kidlington. A large part of the capital was subscribed by the Duke of Marlborough, whose seat was (and continues to be) at Blenheim Palace, and he was also one of the first directors of the company. The branch opened on 19 May 1890 and was worked by the GWR from the outset. In August the same year the GWR obtained powers to extend the branch parallel to the main line at Kidlington for Blenheim. The Woodstock Railway became part of the GWR on 1 July 1897. The branch crossed the River Cherwell twice while running parallel to the main line and one of these crossings was the site of the worst accident in the history of the GWR (it occurred on the main line and not the branch running parallel to it). On Christmas Eve 1874 a wheel of one of the coaches of a London to Birkenhead train fractured and the resulting accident killed thirty passengers and four railwaymen, and seriously injured another sixty-five.

Locomotive No. 1473, 'Fair Rosamund', and carriage No. 119 at Blenheim & Woodstock, 10 May 1930.

The line was worked by the 'one engine in steam' method, there being no crossing place; indeed, there was no intermediate stopping place until the halt at Shipton-on-Cherwell, which served the villages of Shipton and Thrupp, opened on 1 April 1929. The journey took about ten minutes, most services only running to and from Kidlington, although some started and finished in Oxford. Goods services were provided: a path for a goods train was available and one train each way could be run as a mixed train (passenger and goods). In its latter days the line was usually worked by a 57xx class pannier tank with a single autocoach. Sadly, many people from Blenheim preferred the bus but passenger numbers from Shipton-on-Cherwell remained reasonable as the bus services for Shipton and Thrupp were poor. The line did not survive to the Beeching era and although the official closure date was 1 March 1954, as there was no Sunday service the last train ran on 27 February. There was a good crowd to see the last train, which was a two-coach autotrain with loco No. 1420 in the middle. Someone had written the name 'Fair Rosamund' on the loco in remembrance of the one of that name that had worked the branch in the past, No. 1473. Among the passengers was a Mr Caster, then eighty-six, who had worked on the construction of the line and had also travelled on the first train.

Fairford Branch *

	Date			Date
Passenger service withdrawn	18 June 1962		*Stations closed*	
Distance	22.3 miles (Yarnton to Fairford)		South Leigh	18 June 1962
Company	Witney Railway/East Gloucestershire Railway		Witney **	18 June 1962
			Brize Norton & Bampton ***	18 June 1962
			Carterton	18 June 1962
Stations closed	*Date*		Alvescot	18 June 1962
Eynsham	18 June 1962		Kelmscott & Langford	18 June 1962
Cassington Halt	18 June 1962			

Eynsham Station, looking towards Fairford, 1 May 1956.

* Closed stations on this line that were in Gloucestershire were Lechlade and Fairford.
** This station opened on 15 January 1873, replacing an earlier station which had been the terminus of the Witney Railway, when the line was extended to Fairford. The old station remained in use as Witney goods depot.

*** Originally known as Bampton, but renamed Bampton (Oxon) on 2 July 1906 (to distinguish it from Bampton Devon) and given its final name on 1 May 1940.

South Leigh Station, looking towards Fairford, 1 May 1956.

The branch from Yarnton, on the GWR main line from Oxford to Worcester, to Fairford in Gloucestershire was built in two distinct stages. However, there had been long series of proposals, ultimately fruitless, which would have linked Witney to the railway network. The earliest of these had been made in 1836 when there were rival proposals by the GWR and LNWR for a direct line from London to Cheltenham. The LNWR scheme failed to gain parliamentary approval while the GWR scheme went no further. The Oxford, Worcester & Wolverhampton obtained powers for a branch to Witney in 1846, but there matters rested. At a meeting shortly before Christmas 1858, the people of Witney decided to take matters into their own hands and as a result the Witney Railway Bill was presented to Parliament. The GWR opposed the bill as they feared LNWR competition over the line, which might be extended to Cheltenham. Despite this opposition, the bill was passed in August 1859 and the line opened for passenger and coal traffic on 14 November 1861, the station at Yarnton on the main line opening on the same day. Opening for general goods had to wait until March the following year, when the facilities to handle it had been completed. Intermediate stations existed at Eynsham and South Leigh; Cassington Halt did not open until 9 March 1936.

Witney Station.

Services were worked by the West Midland Railway (later the GWR when it absorbed that company). At first there were four trains each day and a small dividend could be paid by the company to shareholders. However, many debts were outstanding, much of the land had not been paid for and revenue did not come up to expectations. Suspicions were raised that the GWR had not been passing on the amounts due to the local company, although nothing was proved. In 1864 the proposal for a more direct line to Cheltenham appeared again in the form of the East Gloucestershire Railway (EGR), from Witney. While the Witney company looked on this – and the increased traffic it was expected to bring – as its salvation, existing financial difficulties became more pressing. In 1867 a receiver was appointed to deal with the outstanding claims for payment for the land used and in 1871 a new working agreement was made with the GWR. The company came out of receivership in 1875 and payment of dividends resumed.

The proposals for the EGR were closely linked with various schemes for a more direct line from London to Cheltenham than via Swindon. These were supported by the people of Cheltenham who wanted better links, and by the LNWR and Midland which were always keen to compete with the GWR. Ultimately, the EGR had to build its line without the support of any of the large companies. It had trouble raising finance and decided to build the Witney to Fairford section first. The line opened on 15 January 1873, with a through service of four trains per day from Oxford, and was worked by the GWR. There were intermediate stations at Bampton, Alvescot and Lechlade. Kelmscott & Langford opened on 4 November 1907, while Carterton opened on 2 October 1944 to serve a nearby American airbase.

Brize Norton & Bampton Station, looking towards Oxford, 4 May 1957.

In that form the East Gloucestershire gave little help to the Witney Railway. The GWR was unlikely to contribute to a through route that would compete with its own route and with the passage of time talk of extensions faded away. In July 1890 the GWR took over both the East Gloucester and the Witney railways and the line settled down as a quiet, and somewhat long, GWR branch. As a footnote to the story of plans to link Cheltenham to London by a more direct route via Oxford, in the 1940s there was a service through Witney (but not Fairford) and Andoversford (GWR station) by bus from Oxford. As the GWR was no longer a bus operator by this time, the buses were operated by the Bristol Tramways and Carriage Co. Ltd. This way, the trip from Paddington to Cheltenham took about 4½ hours compared to about 3½ hours by train via Swindon.

Carterton Station, looking towards Oxford, 1 May 1956.

Services improved over the years and by 1922 there were five through trains daily with an additional two to and from Witney, a third of these being added on Saturdays. There was a Sunday service – only one train each way departing Oxford late in the afternoon at 4:52 p.m. and from Fairford at 6:30 p.m. Journey times were about seventy minutes. There was one through goods service a day with a second one going as far as Witney. Some unusual workings occurred in the autumn when the Witney Blanket Company sent out its products. In 1923 no less than 60,000 blankets were sent and this required special trains of four-wheel vans and could bring unusual locos to the branch; one used in 1923 was 2-4-0 No. 3247. During the 1920s, trains were often in the charge of 2-4-0 Metro tanks while various pannier tanks served the line in its later days.

2251 class No. 2236 with a goods service from Fairford at Alvescot Station, 2 February 1957.

Great Central to Banbury *

Passenger service withdrawn	5 September 1966	Stations closed	Date
Distance	8.25 miles (Culworth Junction to Great Western Junction Banbury)	Chalcombe Road Halt	6 February 1956
Company	Great Central Railway		

* The closed station on this line that was in Northamptonshire was Eydon Road Halt.

The Great Central line to Banbury was opened from Culworth Junction, south of Woodford, on the Great Central main line, on 13 August 1900. Services were provided from Oxford to Leicester. The line joined the GWR main line north of Banbury and then used running powers to run into the GWR station, referred to as Banbury Bridge Street in Bradshaw's timetables (although the GWR just referred to it as Banbury until July 1938 when it was renamed Banbury General). The line was built by the Great Central, but as this company was heavily financially committed in building its London extension, it was loaned the money by the GWR. The two intermediate halts opened later: Chalcombe Road Halt on 17 April 1911 and Eydon Road Halt on 1 October 1913. The line was double track and, besides its local traffic, was important as a through cross-country route. Passenger services included Newcastle to Swansea, Newcastle to Bournemouth and York to Bristol. Goods traffic was also very important over the line and there were extensive marshalling yards at Banbury to handle the re-forming of trains that was required. Much of the Great Central route was closed in 1966 and with it went this route.

Kingham to Banbury

Passenger service withdrawn	Chipping Norton to Banbury: 4 June 1951; Kingham to Chipping Norton: 3 December 1962
Distance	19.95 miles (Kingham to King's Sutton)
Company	Chipping Norton Railway / Banbury & Cheltenham Direct Railway

The signal box at Sarsden Station.

Stations closed	Date
Sarsden Halt *	3 December 1962
Chipping Norton **	3 December 1962
Rollright Halt	4 June 1951
Hook Norton	4 June 1951
Bloxham	4 June 1951
Milton Halt	4 June 1951
Adderbury	4 June 1951

* Originally known as Sarsden Siding which had been in use since July 1897. It was renamed on 2 July 1906.
** This was the second station, opened just north of the earlier one which was the terminus of the Chipping Norton Railway and which closed when the through route was opened.

Sarsden Station, *c*.1909.

ARRIVAL of 3-15 TRAIN SARSDEN HALT

The Banbury & Cheltenham Direct Railway was built in two parts, the first being the section west of Kingham. However, this line lay in Gloucestershire and is outside the scope of this book. The need for a line linking Banbury and Cheltenham had long been felt and there had been a number of proposals to meet that need. One of the earliest, in 1851, was for the Oxford, Worcester & Wolverhampton main line at Moreton-in-Marsh to meet a LNWR branch from Banbury but this did not bear fruit. The Chipping Norton Railway opened on 10 August 1855 (which was a public holiday in Chipping Norton) from a junction on the OW&W Oxford to Worcester main line (which was known as Chipping Norton Junction, despite its proximity to the village of Kingham, until it was renamed in 1909). The contractor was Peto who had contributed three-fifths of the cost of the line. Although a separate company, it was worked by the OW&W from the beginning and was taken over by the GWR in 1863.

In 1864 and 1865 there were no less than four proposals to link Chipping Norton with Banbury, connecting either with the GWR or the LNWR at Banbury or in one instance extending further to a proposed junction at Moreton Pinkney on the East & West Junction Railway (later the Stratford-upon-Avon & Midland Junction Railway). Further schemes were put forward in 1871 and 1873 and in that year the Banbury & Cheltenham Direct Railway was incorporated.

Late in 1874, Edward Wilson was instructed to proceed with construction of the line, a case of tenacity paying off as he had been involved with some of the proposals since 1864. There was a financial crisis in 1878 which led to construction work being suspended and the section from Chipping Norton to King's Sutton did not open until 6 April 1887. Intermediate stations were provided at Chipping Norton, Hook Norton, Bloxham and Adderbury. The halt at Sarsden opened on 2 July 1906, while Rollright Halt opened on 12 December 1906 and Milton Halt on 1 January 1908. The line was worked by the GWR, which took it over in 1897. From the first, expectations for freight traffic over the line, particularly ironstone, were high. Sidings were provided to quarries at Bloxham, Milton and Sydenham, while passing loops and at least two sidings 800 feet in length to accommodate the ironstone traffic were to be provided at every station when the line was built. At one time there were sixteen stone trains daily over the route, but by the mid 1950s there was only one daily goods train between Chipping Norton and Banbury.

An accident involving 0-4-2T locomotive No. 546 at Chipping Norton, 23 May 1907.

The line was worked in two sections, Cheltenham to Kingham and Kingham to Banbury. There were six trains a day from Kingham to Banbury in 1910, all provided by autotrains. In 1922 there was the same weekday service over the length of the line, but Chipping Norton was much better served by a more frequent railmotor service to Kingham. In the last year of GWR services, 1947, there were four through trains over the line but the number of additional trains between Chipping Norton and Kingham had been reduced to only two. It appears that Sundays remained undisturbed by the sound of trains along the route. Passenger services were withdrawn east of Chipping Norton in 1951, leaving only three daily services from Kingham to Chipping Norton.

Rollright Halt.

After the Kingham direct line (providing a direct link between the eastern and western sections and avoiding the need to reverse into Kingham Station) opened in 1906 the line's potential as a through route was greatly enhanced and the Ports to Ports Express between Cardiff and Newcastle was provided from May 1906, being withdrawn in September 1939. At one time this was worked by Castle class locos but later reverted to Moguls (locos of a 2-6-0 wheel arrangement).

Hook Norton Station.

HOOK NORTON.

Hook Norton Station and shed, looking east, *c.*1909.

Bloxham Station, looking towards Chipping Norton, 16 June 1958.

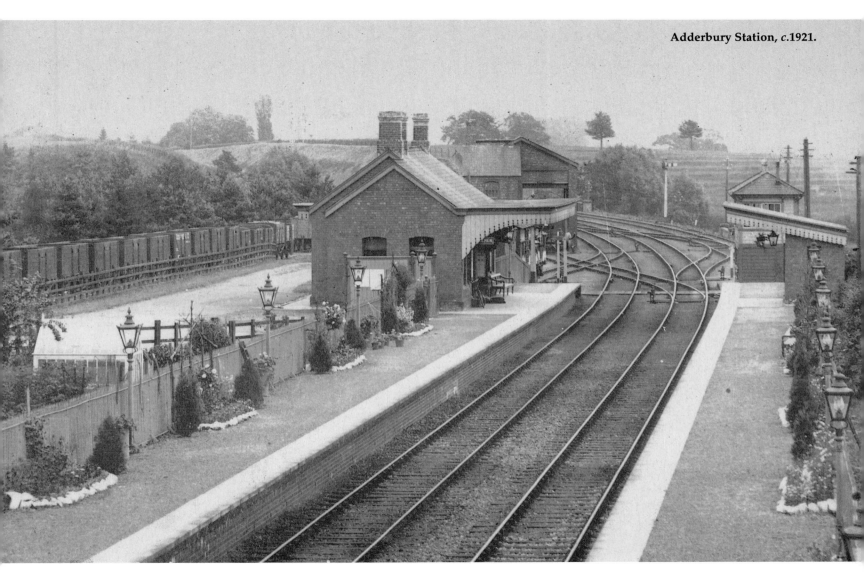

Adderbury Station, *c.*1921.

LNWR to Banbury *

Passenger service withdrawn	2 January 1961		*Stations closed*	*Date*
Distance	30.5 miles (Bletchley to Banbury)		Banbury Merton Street **	2 January 1961
Company	Buckinghamshire Railway			

* Closed stations on this line in Northamptonshire were Farthinghoe and Brackley, while the line's closed stations in Buckinghamshire were Fulwell & Westbury, Buckingham, Padbury, Verney Junction, Winslow and Swanbourne.

** This station was originally known as Banbury L&NW but had changed to Banbury Merton Street by April 1910.

Banbury Merton Street Station, 8 March 1956.

The Buckinghamshire Railway was formed by amalgamation of the Oxford & Bletchley Junction and the Buckingham & Brackley Junction railways. It joined the LNWR main line at Bletchley and split at Verney Junction, the southerly line going to Oxford while the northerly one went to Brackley. The Act of amalgamation also provided for an extension northwards from Brackley to Banbury. The line to Banbury opened for passengers on 1 May 1850 (about nine months before the GWR) and for goods two weeks later. Although an independent company, the Buckinghamshire Railway was regarded as being strategically important by the LNWR (in that it might have formed the basis for further extensions to the west) and it contributed more than half its capital. It was always worked by the LNWR, which took a 999-year lease on the line in July 1851 and absorbed it in July 1879. In June 1872 the Northampton & Banbury Junction Railway opened as far as a junction with the LNWR Banbury line at Cockley Brake and then used running powers over the LNWR line into Banbury. It was bought by the Stratford-upon-Avon & Midland Junction Railway in July 1910. The S&MJR became part of the LMS at the Grouping.

Banbury Merton Street Station, 15 March 1952.

In 1910 the service was three trains per day to and from Northampton (with an extra one on Thursdays). The LNWR service from Bletchley had four down trains (to Banbury), including a through coach from Euston by the 4:05 p.m. train which was slipped at Bletchley. There were five up trains and the 9:40 a.m. included a through coach for London. Sundays saw one return train a day. In 1922 there were only two daily S&MJ trains; the LNWR service remained about the same although by then the through London coach had gone and the Sunday service now had two trains each way. The Northampton service was withdrawn in July 1951. As an experiment to cut costs and boost revenues on the line, diesel railcar operation was introduced in 1956 and at the same time two new halts were opened. As was so often the case, the improvements were not as great as had been hoped. It had been intended to withdraw the passenger service on 4 January 1960, but because an adequate replacement bus service was not available the service was reprieved until the end of the year. The service was officially withdrawn from 2 January 1961, but as there was no Sunday service the last train ran on 31 December 1960.

Oxford to Princes Risborough *

Passenger service withdrawn	7 January 1963		
Distance	18.6 miles (junction at Princes Risborough		
	to Kennington Junction, Oxford)		
Company	Wycombe Railway		

Stations closed	*Date*
Iffley Halt	22 March 1915

Stations closed	*Date*
Littlemore	7 January 1963
Morris Cowley **	7 January 1963
Horspath Halt ***	7 January 1963
Wheatley	7 January 1963
Tiddington	7 January 1963
Thame	7 January 1963

Morris Cowley Station, looking towards Thame, 9 November 1957.

MORRIS COWLEY

PASSENGERS ARE NOT ALLOWED TO CROSS THE RAILWAY

* Closed stations on this line that were in Buckinghamshire were Bledlow and Towersey.
** This was previously the site of Garsington Bridge Halt which closed on 22 March 1915 and reopened with its new name on 24 September 1928.
*** This was the second halt of this name and opened on 5 June 1933. The first one was a few yards to the west and had opened on 1 February 1908 and closed on 22 March 1915.

Horspath Halt, looking towards Oxford, 9 November 1957.

The Wycombe Railway set out to link Maidenhead with High Wycombe. Unlike many smaller railways which failed to achieve their promoters' ambitions, the Wycombe Railway, once it had achieved its initial aim, looked for fresh areas to expand into. It got to Princes Risborough and then built lines to Aylesbury and Oxford. It is the latter that concerns us here. Despite objections from the West Midland Railway, which hoped to build a separate route to London through the area, parliamentary powers for the line were granted by an Act of June 1861. The Midland also had designs on the area and planned a line from London to Cheltenham that would have passed through it and used the Witney and East Gloucestershire railways to gain access to Cheltenham.

The broad gauge line was opened to Thame on 1 August 1862 and to Oxford on 24 October 1864. Intermediate stations were provided at Littlemore, Wheatley, Tiddington, Thame and Bledlow. The halts at Iffley, Garsington Bridge and Horspath opened on 1 February 1908 in conjunction with the new railmotor service, which was intended to stimulate traffic on the line. The Wycombe Railway had always been worked by the GWR and this arrangement continued until it was absorbed by that company in 1867. The gauge was narrowed between 23 August and 1 September 1870.

Tiddington Station, looking towards Oxford, 16 June 1957.

At the beginning of the twentieth century the GWR planned a shorter route to Birmingham and it achieved this, in part, by building a joint line with the Great Central Railway, which was in the process of building its London extension. This resulted in a route from Paddington to Oxford via the Wycombe Railway that was 8 miles shorter than via Didcot, but the line's services were always local in nature. There was a direct service from Paddington via Denham and Princes Risborough to Oxford but it ambled along, stopping at every station along the line (and most of those between Paddington and Princes Risborough as well), taking about 2½ hours for a journey of 55 miles. Oxford trains via Didcot varied a lot in speed but in 1922 the 4:45 p.m. Hereford express (complete with 'Tea Car') took one hour and ten minutes non-stop for the 63½ mile journey.

Thame Station, *c.*1913.

The branch service in 1922 consisted of six through trains daily, taking about fifty minutes for the journey, with an extra one on Tuesdays and two workings from Princes Risborough to Thame and back. On Sundays the line had two through workings in each direction. After the railmotors ceased running, autotrains ran on the branch and in the 1950s GWR-built diesel railcars could also be seen on the branch. There is an interesting reference to one of these breaking down in Horspath Tunnel and having to be rescued by the steam loco of a following freight train in July 1955. Larger locos such as members of the Hall class could also be seen on the line.

Watlington Branch *

			Stations closed	Date
Passenger service withdrawn	1 July 1957		Chinnor	1 July 1957
Distance	8.8 miles		Kingston Crossing Halt	1 July 1957
Company	Watlington & Princes Risborough Railway		Aston Rowant	1 July 1957
			Lewknor Bridge Halt	1 July 1957
* Closed stations on this line that were in Buckinghamshire were			Watlington	1 July 1957
Wainhill Halt and Bledlow Bridge Halt.				

Chinnor Station.

Kingston Crossing Halt, looking towards Princes Risborough, 12 June 1957.

An early scheme to put Watlington on the railway map was the Wallingford & Watlington Railway which planned to build a line from Cholsey, on the GWR main line to Bristol, to a junction with the Wycombe Railway. Only the first section, from Cholsey to Wallingford was built. The residents of Watlington were not pleased at this and floated their own scheme, the Watlington & Princes Risborough Railway. This concern obtained its Act in 1869 for a line from a separate station in Princes Risborough to a station at Watlington some three-quarters of a mile from the town centre. This was not terribly convenient for the town but was close to Shirburn Castle, seat of the Earl of Macclesfield who was one of several prominent Watlington people among the directors.

Aston Rowant Station, 16 August 1919.

The line was built as cheaply as possible and as a result it followed the contours of the land closely, in a way foreshadowing later light railways. It opened on 15 August 1872. There were two intermediate stations, Aston Rowant and Chinnor, but neither were crossing places and the line was worked on the 'one engine in steam' basis, despite a promise having been made to the Board of Trade to use the 'staff and ticket' system. The initial service was three trains a day but the line was so poorly used that it was soon in financial difficulties and the directors had to put their hands into their own pockets to keep it going. Locomotives and rolling stock were hired from the Great Western but later the Watlington Rolling Stock Co. was formed to hire rolling stock to the W&PRR. The company was soon in disagreement with the GWR over the junction at Princes Risborough and by October 1876 the sum of £2,000 was owed to the larger company. A new, five year, agreement was put in place later that year. The company chairman, a Mr Taylor, was unhappy at the amount of money he had lent the company and started discussions with Sir Daniel Gooch, GWR, to work the line and later take it over. At first the GWR was unenthusiastic and would not consider the suggested extensions to Didcot, Reading or Wallingford. After prolonged negotiations the GWR took over the line on 1 June 1883, taking formal possession on 31 December that year. The purchase price was less than half the cost of constructing the line.

Lewknor Bridge Halt.

The GWR takeover did not go smoothly; Taylor was as obstructive as possible, the plans and sections of the line were not handed over, and as no proper land conveyances had been drawn up when the line was being built (receipts only having been used) the GWR later had difficulty over the title of the land. Services were improved when railmotors were introduced in 1906 and additional halts were opened on 1 September that year at Bledlow Bridge, Kingston Crossing and Lewknor Bridge. The halt at Wainhill opened on 1 August 1925. Watlington had its own loco shed until it was destroyed by fire. After that the branch engine was stabled overnight over the loco pit, until, that is, the fireman was called up for his national service. As no replacement for him could be found in Watlington, the loco and crew had to come a considerable distance every day, departing Slough 'light engine' at 5:38 a.m. to arrive at Watlington at 7 a.m. The return journey at the end of the day took almost two hours. In the line's early days locos and rolling stock were provided by the GWR. The Watlington Rolling Stock Co. used two locos, a Sharp Stewart 2-2-2WT which was probably not well suited to the gradients of the branch and a 2-4-0T, also by Sharp Stewart. This was rebuilt by the GWR and later sold to Colonel Stephens for use on the Weston Clevedon & Portishead line, where it was named 'Hesperus'. In its last days the line was generally worked by pannier tanks of the 57xx class but 14xx autotanks could occasionally be seen.

In 1922 the service consisted of five return trains a day, except Sundays, taking about 25 minutes for the journey in each direction. In that year the branch had two through workings from Paddington, slip coaches being provided on the 9:10 a.m. and 7:10 p.m. departures from there. Just before closure, the service consisted of five trains from Watlington and four from Princes Risborough, with an extra return working on Saturdays. One train from Princes Risborough ran as an empty stock working, although it is said that passengers who turned up were normally carried. Passenger services were withdrawn from 1 July 1957, but as there was no Sunday service the last trains ran on Saturday 29 June. This was not the end of the line as goods and parcels services continued at Aston Rowant, Chinnor and Watlington (although services beyond Chinnor were finally withdrawn from 2 January 1961). Goods services continued for the 3¾ miles to Chinnor to serve the Chinnor Cement Works, coal for the process being brought in by rail until ceasing in December 1989. The line from Chinnor to Princes Risborough is now part of a preservation scheme.

Closed passenger stations on lines still open to passengers

Line/service   **Great Western: West of England main line**

Stations closed	*Date*
Goring *	29 February 1892

* This station, opened on 1 June 1840, was replaced by a new station that opened on the day the old one closed.

Line/service   **Oxford, Worcester & Wolverhampton line**

Stations closed	*Date*
Yarnton *	18 June 1962

* This was the junction for the Fairford line.

Yarnton Station.

Line/service	**Great Western: Didcot to Warwick**	Stations closed	Date
		Wolvercot Platform	1 January 1916
Stations closed	Date	Kidlington for Blenheim **	2 November 1964
Abingdon Road Halt	22 March 1915	Bletchington ***	2 November 1964
Hinksey Halt	22 March 1915	Fritwell and Somerton ****	2 November 1964
Oxford *	1 October 1852	Cropredy	17 September 1956

Abingson Road Halt.

* This station was replaced on its date of closure by the second station when the line was extended to the north of Oxford. It remained in use for goods until November 1872.

** This station was known as Woodstock Road until 19 May 1890 when the Blenheim & Woodstock Branch opened, but for a short time before July 1855 was known as Langford Lane.

*** From its opening in September 1850 until May 1851 this was simply known as Woodstock and then as Woodstock Road until July 1855 (when Langford Lane to the south was named Woodstock Road). It was then known as Kirtlington until 11 August 1890.

**** This station was known as Somerton (Oxon) between July 1906 and 1 October 1907 (to distinguish it from Somerton (Somerset)). Prior to that it had simply been known as Somerton from its opening in 1855.

Bletchington Station.

Fritwell & Somerton Station.

Line/service	Stations closed	Date
Great Western main line to Birmingham	Blackthorn	8 June 1953
	Ardley *	7 January 1963

Blackthorn Station.

* This station was downgraded to halt status on 1 August 1955.

Castle class 4-6-0 No. 5087, 'Tintern Abbey', at Blackthorn Station, 19 April 1957.

Ardley Station, *c.*1910.

Line/service	**Great Central London extension**

Stations closed	Date
Finmere *	4 March 1963

* This station was originally known as Finmere for Buckingham but had been renamed by 1922.

Line/service	**LNWR to Oxford**

Stations closed	Date
Oxford Rewley Road *	1 October 1951
Port Meadow Halt (a) **	25 October 1926
Wolvercote Halt (a)	25 October 1926

Stations closed	Date
Oxford Road Halt (a) ***	25 October 1926
Oddington Halt (a) ****	25 October 1926
Charlton Halt (a)	25 October 1926
Wendlebury Halt (a)	25 October 1926
Launton	1 January 1968

Oxford Rewley Road Station.

(a) These halts were closed between 1 January 1917 and 5 May 1919.
* From 1 October 1951 trains were diverted from here to the GWR station. The LNWR station has gone on to another life, being dismantled and rebuilt at Quainton Road, Buckinghamshire where it provides magnificent accommodation.

** Known as Summertown Halt until 1 January 1907.
*** Initially known as Oxford Road and closed on 20 May 1851. It reopened as Oxford Road Halt on 20 October 1905.
**** Originally opened on 1 October 1850 as Oddington and closed in January 1851. It reopened as Oddington Halt on 20 October 1905.

Renown class 4-4-0 No. 1936, 'Royal Sovereign',
piloting the 2-4-0 locomotive 'Wyre' with a
down train passing Port Meadow Halt.

The site of Oddington Halt, looking towards Bicester, 16 February 1958.

A new rail motor at Wendlebury Halt.